AF350712

I Am Disturbed

Deep Inside
the Real Diary of a Teenage Girl

While every precaution has been taken in the preparation of this book, the publisher assumes no responsibility for errors or omissions, or for damages resulting from the use of the information contained herein.

I AM DISTURBED DEEP INSIDE THE REAL DIARY OF A TEENAGE GIRL

First edition. June 1, 2024.

Copyright © 2024 Isabel Fe.

ISBN: 979-8224118861

Written by Isabel Fe.

Table of Contents

I Am Disturbed Deep Inside the Real Diary of a Teenage Girl.........1

Introduction 2

Chapter One...4

Chapter Two...7

Chapter Three 11

Chapter Four 14

Chapter Five 16

Chapter Six 20

Chapter Seven 25

Chapter Eight... 37

Chapter Nine.. 46

Chapter Ten 54

Chapter Eleven... 59

Chapter Twelve... 62

Chapter Thirteen 75

Chapter Fourteen 84

Written by Isabel Fe Illustration by Michelle Franklin

A 10% PORTION OF THE proceeds from this book will be donated to SPTS (The Society of the Prevention of Teen Suicide) which provides awareness, resources and advocacy for the prevention of teenage suicide. For more information visit website at: https://sptsusa.org/

Introduction

05/22/97

As you read my journal, I hope that it will give inspiration and hope to anyone struggling to make sense of this life. Between my twisted journal entries to my erotic poetry that you can taste on the tip of your tongue to my ex-boyfriend's letters, this is my real journal, starting at the age of 15, pouring my heart out and spilling it on to this, that once was an ordinary, white, blank piece of paper.

Isabel,
I bought this for you because you always seem to have something to write. Now you can get rid of the notebooks and let your pen's ink flow in here. I guess basically, when there isn't anyone to listen, let the book be your friend!
Love ya always,
Jenny

Chapter One

Now that I finally have a journal to write in, I'm going to jot down some notes that I had written on separate sheets of paper. These are very important to me, and I would never want to lose them. Well, I was going to write a poem, but I think I can express my words better in a note. It's late and I have to wake up for school in 5 hours. I can't seem to get to sleep. I'm lying here with a pen and some paper with a flashlight on. I'm terrified of being alone in the darkness when it's silent, so I had to do something. Everything in my life is going wrong. The only thing I seem to care about lately is Ryan. I think I've already lost Jenny. It's not the same as it used to be. Well ever since we started disagreeing about Ryan. She doesn't think I should be doing the things that we're doing together, let alone talk to him. Neither do I. I just can't seem to let him go. He has ruined my whole life ever since I met him. Actually, it's because I let him. I'm so ashamed of myself because of it. I've been very depressed to the point where I've had thoughts of suicide. My grades haven't been the best since 8th grade. That leads me to no future. I hate feeling sorry for myself like this. I have no one to turn too anymore. It used to be Jenny, but she doesn't want to listen or pay any attention to the subject, thinking that it's just a phase I'm going through and that I'll get over it but the truth is that I've been going through this ever since the 7th grade-since I met Ryan-and I can't deal with it anymore. I hate living like this. And now I think that I'm finally over him because of Cole. But then I go and fuck up that relationship too. I can't believe I was so stupid to go and mess around with Ryan at the same time I was with Cole. Just last night Cole and I were talking on the phone, and he started crying because I confessed to him about me and Ryan. He cried over me? Why? I don't deserve anything. Why does he care for a person like me who has so much hatred in her? I'm starting to mess up his life too. Why does everything that's good for me go wrong all of the time? I'm so scared to fall in love with someone else again. Cole has already broken my heart twice, so why should I give him another chance, so he can do the same thing all over to me again? I think I lost him last night.

And my family, well let's see, I treat my mom like shit. I never tell her how much I appreciate all of the things she's done for me. I have caused her and my stepdad so much shit in the past two years. I'm not a good daughter. I expect them to give me everything I want and yet what do I give them in return? Nothing. That's the same for my sister. I've also lost my dad a long time ago. I miss him so much. We used to be so close and now I dread even seeing him anymore. I've caused that whole family lots of heartache too. When I lived there at the beginning of 9th grade, until I left, I thought I had everything. But I really didn't have anything at all. They gave me everything I wanted except for the thing I really needed the most, my father's love. For my birthday this year, I got a pair of earrings that I know my stepmom picked out. What I really wanted was for my dad to give me a big hug and a kiss and tell me how much he loves me, even though I've been a pain in the ass. And even though I left the way I did. I wanted something that would mean something to me. Well, I gotta go. I'll continue this page tomorrow.

Well, I'm back. It's tomorrow. Cole came over today, and I think everything is going pretty well between us. Ryan called me again and of course I called him back. Why did I do that? It's like I have another personality. I'm so confused. There's no way I can do this to Cole again. I care about him a hell of a lot more than I do for Ryan. Cole is supposed to call when he gets home. I know he will. I can rely on him at any time. I just hope everything can work out between us. I doubt it though. He probably has this plan to dump me at any chance he can get. I hope he goes to my sister's wedding. Then everything will go as I planned. Well, I gotta go. See ya!

Chapter Two

Letters from Ryan

Isabel,

Hey bitch, what's up? So, you know what, fuck you. J/K about the bitch part. So whatcha up too? Me, not too much. Just sitting in my room, thinking of ya (only because I'm writin you). Do you know that teasing guys is wrong? So, hope you have fun on your little trip. Well, I gotta go. Cya. Sorry so sloppy.

W/B/N (write back now),

Ryan

Your eyes only. Fuck you. So, what's up with Saturday if you want. Call me tonight. P.S. I had a dream about you last night.

Ryan

Isabel,

Hey girl, whuz up? Not too much here. Just sittin in English writin you. Well, you can go as far as you want. I mean it's your life and your relationship and I don't have anything to do with either right? Well, I hope I do. So, well you're right. I had no fucking idea what you were talking about in your note. It was tooooooooooooooooo confusing. All my brains are at my nuts. So, I'm confused. What did you mean? Did it mean you're not gonna tease me anymore or you are? Anywayz. So, you let me go to write Cole? I see how you are. Why you gotta be sooo mean, huh? From now on, I'm gonna tease you if you don't stop teasing me. So how far are you gonna go with Cole tonight? I hope not too far because I don't want you falling in love with him, because if you did, there'd be none left for me. Well, I'm gonna let you go so I can go write

no one.

Cya around,

Ryan

I,

Hey little girl. Was up? Not too much here. Just sittin in science class writing you. So, how's your day been? The way I heard it, not so good so far. Well two more days till ya know. So, are you looking forward to it? Well, I guess I am. The other night, I had another dream about you, but it wasn't that long. Maybe I'll tell you about it later. So, what'll happen with you and Cole? What did you tell him? Well, I'll write you a longer note later, but you better write me a longer one back.

Cya,

Ryan

Isabel,

Hey girl. Whuz up? Not too much here, just sitting in English class writin you. So, did you dream about me or what? You better have because if you didn't, I'll beat your ass. So, what else do you want for your birthday? Well, I'll explain that dream to you some other time maybe later today. We'll see. If I meet you today after school, I'll show you my dream. Ok you better not have that bad of a hangover on Saturday or I'll beat your ass, literally. So anyway, well I guess you'll get something more for your birthday because you're so special. What do you want? Well, I gotta let you go, getting tired of writing. I'll write ya later.

C-ya.

Call me when you get home.

Ryan

Chapter Three

Thoughts

Just laying here, thinking again. I wish I had someone to write this too, but I don't, so I guess this is another journal entry. I always seem to look back at my past and of all the bad memories. I can't help but to wonder why I never look back at the good memories of my past and know that they're there but then look ahead into the future. Maybe it's because there's more of the bad than of the good. And some of those thoughts go back to when I was daddy's little girl and everything in my life couldn't be better. No worries, no heartbreak, nothing. Just plain old-fashioned love between a father and a daughter. Now that I've grown up a bit, I know that he can't give me the attention that he used to give to me. He has a family of his own that he must take care of. But every day I want to know why he has changed so much in the process of doing so. Has she changed him into this man? A man I used to call my daddy but now he's just my father. I love him so much but yet I don't know if he loves me? I should already know but it's sad to say that I really don't know anymore. I lost the trust, the love, and the loyalty that we once had. When it was just us. But now I know I will never again in this lifetime, have the chance to be alone with just him, to have a whole day to spend with him. Time is too short. Somebody always has something more important to do to keep us busy. All of this that's running through my mind still leads me to believe that's the reason I've gotten so boy crazy, so obsessed with having a relationship with a guy, so interested in a guy that uses me for sex, is all because of not having a stable relationship with my father. I don't do any of this on purpose...how I get into so much trouble. Maybe it's because I expect my mom to give me not only her full attention, but also my fathers' and that's not fair. I really do believe that there is another person inside of me when I get into trouble. I don't know, but whatever it is, I am going to need someone to talk to real soon about all of this. I need some advice from somebody. Oh, what am I going to do without Mrs. Jacobson in junior high school? She is the only person in this whole world that really knows me, not only as a person, but knows part of me inside. No one else would understand the things that I would say to them. She knows what my point of view is. What I've been through. I wish I could've thanked her for all that she's done for me in the past 3 years. I owe her my life. She has saved me and helped me through so much. She is a very wonderful person. Well, I have to go now. I'm pretty tired.

Just sitting here listening to music. I'm in another one of those thinking moods again. I haven't talked to Cole in two days. Why hasn't he tried to call me? Sometimes I feel like complete shit because of him. Maybe I just need some reassurance. I miss him so much. He's leaving tomorrow for vacation, and we won't talk to each other for a week. I guess this will really prove how much we like being together because I'll be ungrounded the whole time he's gone. I just don't know how I can live with myself. I've kept so many secrets from him and only half-truths have been told. I don't deserve him right now. It's amazing how quickly the story can change or switch places. Maybe I should just break up with him. I'm going to be in high school next year and everything is going to change. I know it. It's just so hard to say the exact words in a way that he'll still be my friend. For only being 15, my life has gotten way too complicated already. I just don't know how to handle anything by myself without someone there to help or guide me along. I guess that's another part of growing up and facing reality. Ryan deserves everything I've done to him recently. I could have never imagined in my past, that I could love someone so much and have that feeling turn into hate. I mean I'll always love him. He took something away from me that meant a lot and I'm glad we've shared those special experiences together, but me pushing him out of my life is just another part of growing up. Maybe he'll learn a lesson from all of this. Never take advantage of a girl's love for him because what comes around goes around. He's going to have to do a little growing up himself too. I'm glad we've gone through so much in the 3 years I've known him. I hope that feeling is mutual, even though it all doesn't mean as much to him as it did to me. I have to go now. I'll finish later.

Chapter Four

Letters from Cole

Isabel,

Hey girl, what's up? Not much here. Just sitting here doing nothing, except writing you. This teacher is the best. I should ask him for a smoke. Well anyway, how are you today? I'm fine, I guess. I did not want to get up today. I hate rainy days. Isabel, you're a crybaby. Just kidding. You're my baby, right? Anywayz, what couldn't you tell me last night when we were on the phone? You better tell me or I'm going to get mad. So, do you still want to go out this weekend? Anywayz, why don't you where your hair like that all the time, like you have it today? You look damn good today. But I'm not saying that you don't look good all the time. P.S. what are you doing Friday? I was wondering if you want to go to the movies or something? Or you can just come over and we'll rent a movie or something?

Love,

Cole

Isabel,

Hey girl, what's up? Not too much here. Just sitting here, doing nothing except writing you. I'm in the lunchroom right now. We can't even fucking talk in here. So how are you today? I'm sorry if I got you mad in any way. I just think I need you back, that's it. But it is all up to you. Think about it ok? But anyway, are we going to the movies this weekend or not? You're coming over this weekend, ok? I have to stay for 30 mins after school today. So, I will call you when I get home. Anyways, it would be better if you came over Friday because I have baseball practice on Saturday. So, if you can, I want you to come over. Well, time is getting short, so gotta go, see ya. P.S. call me

Love Always,

Cole

Chapter Five

Confusion

Now I'm back. It's midnight. Cole is leaving this morning. I can't talk right now. I'll end up crying myself to sleep instead. Bye.

Now that I've lost everything and everyone that I love, I have to leave. This world has no need for me. I'm sick of my life. I always am disappointing someone. I've caused too much heartache. Maybe I'll live in a better place or maybe I'll suffer in Hell. Whatever happens, I will deserve it. I know I will miss you all very much and I'm sorry this has to happen this way, but life isn't always fair. I've found that out myself. Don't think of this as a suicide note, cause that's not what it's all about. I guess I'm very selfish cause it's mostly about me and what I've done. All of my faults, no one caused. I fucked up all on my own. I regret so much for the age that I am. I shouldn't have this much hurt and pain inside of me, but I do. I can't smile away my tears any longer. I've felt sorry for myself for too long...

Getting ready to leave tonight for the first night of being ungrounded, finally. Ryan still thinks that I'm pregnant. I'm trying to decide if I should let him suffer a little longer or if I should call him and tell him the truth. I finally got in the standing position of our relationship. I'm not falling anymore. Right now, I know he's pissing in his pants! Ha, ha...I love it. This isn't even all for what he's done to me but what he's done to so many other girls too. I keep trying to tell myself that I have Cole, but it's not working very well. I don't want to hurt him. I know the way to tell him though. It would be to his face, and I would tell him that, "I still want to be friends with you. This isn't your fault; our relationship is going great right now. Way better than the other ones we had. But I don't deserve you because I promised myself I wouldn't, but I did. Four days after we started going out again, I cheated on you with Ryan. I'm really sorry it had to end like this." I really do believe that the only reason he asked me out again is because he wants something from me. Sex or revenge. I won't give him the chance for either. Maybe he really does care about me more than I think. He called me Friday night and left a message on my answering machine. Then I actually talked to him on Saturday morning for 30 minutes. He said he tried to call Thursday night, but no one answered. We are both getting along really well. Our phone conversations went really well and our whole relationship is going great. I'm just so afraid of that possibility that he could break-up with me again or cheat on me for revenge. The closer we get, the more scared I get. We are getting a lot closer to each other, just like I've always wanted us to get. He has grown-up since I first have known him at the beginning of this year, and I truly believe that I had something to do with that. I made him realize that if he wants to hang out with me, he's going to have to act more mature. Things have been getting back to normal today. I got my first job. I hope that it works out and I'm sure everyone will be pleased about that. Especially my father. I know my sister freaked. Well, that's some of my thoughts. No one can imagine how much more I could write, but unfortunately there isn't enough time for that. Talk later.

Me and Cole broke up. Actually, I broke up with him. I keep trying to decide if I did the right thing. He deserves someone better than me. I totally cheated on him, and he was faithful to me. I just hope that he'll forgive and forget and at least remain friends with me. We've gone through too much this year not to be. Why doesn't he see that? I know he still cares about me. I just wish he wouldn't be so cold to me. I still care about him, but us being together just isn't going to work out. It's like we'd make great siblings. I don't know. I have to get to bed because Jenny and I are going to Great America tomorrow! We're going to have fun. Bye!

I spent some time with Cole today. He seemed pretty happy to be with me. I just wish it could be mutual. I mean don't get me wrong, he is a really good friend to me, but I think I can finally let go of him. Ryan is in Pennsylvania right now. I hope he forgets about me and doesn't call. I'm always better without him around.

Just sitting here in my room. Another lonely, sad, depressing day. Why can't I just be a normal happy teenager? Everyone I start to give my heart out too...they always leave me or never have time for me. I just don't understand. I've always been like this. I've always been sad about something. From my father to guys to friends to just life in general. I can't deal with it anymore. I'll be gone soon. Nobody needs me that much here. Or at least it seems that way. They never show it. I deserve to die. I've caused so many people so much hurt and pain. I just don't know what to do anymore. There's no other solution. No one is there holding out their hand and helping me. I'll be a faint memory of some people's minds. They all hate me anyway. They all talk about me. I can't stand it anymore... I'll be gone soon.

I just got done reading this whole diary. Wow! I can't believe all of the stuff I've written. Saturday night, I went to Cole's. Everything was fine until I was determined to tell him the truth about what's been going on with me and Ryan. Now I know he'll probably never talk to me again. I hurt him too bad this time. I'm going to call him in a week or so. That's hopefully enough time to let him cool off. Well to finish the story, he got really pissed off and I just walked out. Three guys started following me and I just kept on walking to my house. They left by the time I was at Butterfield's restaurant. I got home, told my ma and she grounded me for walking alone in the dark. I called Cole that night, just to tell him that I got home alright and that I could've gotten raped. I can't believe he let me walk home all by myself. That really shows that he cared about me. Yeah right. Well Ryan called me today. I can't believe I even said what I said! I'm so proud of myself. I told him I didn't want to have sex with him anymore. He seemed kind of stunned that I actually told him what my feelings are instead of just agreeing with what he's feeling at the time. The next time I talk to him is going to be to tell him that the only way we're ever going to have sex again is if we start an actual relationship. I know he'll never say yes to that, so everything will be over. Hopefully.

Well, Ryan came over yesterday, after me telling him I don't want to fool around anymore. I got in trouble. I had to lie again. Too myself also. I hate myself. I have no self-respect. I'll be gone soon, so none of this will matter. Cole hates me. He doesn't care about me after what I did to him. I don't blame him for that. I have to go.

Chapter Six

Disturbed
07/18/96
"Forgotten"
In my mind, they take away my thoughts
In my sleep, they take away my dreams
In my heart, they take away my love
And in my soul, they take me away.
As the days go by slowly,
I think about them
I dream about them
I give them my heart and soul
In my own world, I make it by, just to make it by
I hide my real fears that kill me inside
That's when I'm alone
I smile to cover up the tears
In their minds, I take away their dishonesty
In their sleep, I take away their nightmares
In their hearts, I take away their hate
And in their souls, I give them a stronger one
But as the days go by for them without me
They don't think of me
They don't dream of me
And they give their heart and soul to someone else
I am a simple memory that has been forgotten.

I know you want to love me. I know you want to hold me. You're just too scared. Whenever you decide to come forward and tell me that you care, you go ahead cause I'll be there. The dreams I have about you, make me think that you're just like the rest. I know I care for you, but you treat me bad when we're together. As friends, you treat me like how I want to be treated. I'll admit, we're not going to have this long-lasting relationship, unless you fall in love with me. I hope that in the future, whatever you want you get. I know I won't be there to help you up off your knees. But once you've received what you wanted, I hope you take good care of her and never take her for granted. You'll always be a part of my heart and I'll always love you as a friend. Good luck to you and may you have your wishes and dreams come true.

Love,
Isabel

03/26/96
When I look at you
I see so much
The reflection of myself I have yet to touch
You seem to be so hidden
What are you hiding from?
My secrets are kept within to prevent any pain
Is that sane?
Friends in the past
Now searching for a star
Wishing for hope
Mistakes are forgiven
And now have been forgotten
And the lasting love lingers.

May 1996
"You'll Get By"
Obsessed with my fears
Hiding behind you without a reason
Love me, trust me
Take my hand and fly with me
Not much time before I'm gone forever
No time for pain
No time to suffer
I'm calling your name, a cry for help
Wanting to live, but I'm dying anyway
The need of having someone to hold in my bleeding arms
I'm suffocating
I'm terrified of you
The choice to live or die
Start falling, I'll catch you but not myself
The truth has been twisted into lies
Just to have you both
You'll never understand, no one will
Anger, heartache, all in between the ruins
Afterward, forgive me then forget me
You'll get by without me.

07/18/96

How can I get by without having a part of you? I haven't been able to let you go, how is it easy for you? Saying goodbye to you would be like taking my heart away from me. I can't describe the feeling inside of me. You are everything. I'll always love you. There's no doubt about that. That's the only thing I've been sure about in my entire life. I understand that you don't feel the same way but why have you taken it for granted? Why can't you let me go after all this time? I don't deserve all of this. I deserve better for myself. But what if I never fall in love with anybody else but you? What will I do then? I can't stand this blindness that you see. I'm right here, give me a chance. I know you could fall in love with me. We've known each other for so long, but yet we really don't know each other's minds. You know I love you and I know you don't, so what can I do to forget about you? I want to be in love with someone who loves me too.

08/27/96

Tonight, is the night that I'm deciding to be gone from this world forever. No one can stop me. No one can stand in my way. I'm going to miss you all, but I can no longer stay here. It's as if the devil sent me. God wouldn't allow me to do all the wrong I've done. I'll be praying that he will forgive me of my sins. I will deserve whatever consequences that will happen to me. I love you all and I will keep a part of all of you in my heart. Please forgive me of this and remember only the good memories we have shared. I can't live like this any longer. I can't turn back. I can't change my mind now. It's already too late. Goodbye and I love you all.

Love,

Isabel

Chapter Seven

Hope & Strength
09/06/96

As you can see, I'm still here. I couldn't go through with it. Some force pulled me from doing it. Or maybe I'm too strong to do it. But all I know is that I'm done having those thoughts. My life isn't all that bad. I could have it a lot worse. I'm just thankful that I have what I have. That was stupid and immature of me to think like that. I know that a lot of people care about me and need me in this world. I don't know why I was so depressed, but the fact is that I'm not anymore! I thank God for helping me every step of the way because without him, I don't think I would've made it. I am a true 100% believer now. Who knows why I had doubts before, but I've overcome that too. It feels good to have all of that weight off my shoulders. Once I'm ungrounded, a lot of things are going to change about me. I'm going to try my hardest to become a better person for not only myself but for the people around me. It feels so good to be a happy normal person again. I know I'll still have my ups and downs, but everything will turn out alright, no matter how hard and tough it seems. I'm glad that I went through this experience because it taught me a lot of things and made me more of a person. I'm sure a lot of other teenagers go through the same silly trials and tribulations as I went through. I know I'm not alone. As for what's actually going on in my life, I love high school! I'm having a lot of fun there. My studies are really easy for me because I'm paying lots of attention in class and I'm taking it very seriously. I'm working as hard as I can and trying my best, which is a lot. The classes that I thought would be the hardest, are actually easier than my other classes. I'm joining Drama club, which is going to be so much fun. I know it. And next week is this Expo thing during Team to see what else there is to join. I figure the more you get into school, the more fun you'll get out of it. I want to get a job, but that won't be for a little while. As far as guys in my life, there's really only one that I'm interested in. I met him on vacation with Jenny this summer. He's 16 and drives! Pretty hot too! I've gotten to know him mostly over the phone. He came down once to see me, but it wasn't for more than an hour. He's really nice and has a great personality. He seems interested in me for me and nothing more. I'm making sure of that this time. I can't wait to see him again. Other than that, that's about all the new things in my life. I'm making sure that I don't make guys a major issue this year, cause they come last. Well, I really have to go. Talk later.

Love,
Isabel

09/17/96

A group of us went to Great America on Sunday. I had lots of fun. But my friend Greg was getting jealous of me and this new guy because we were flirting and holding hands and stuff and so Greg was acting like a total dick lately. He's totally obsessed with me. I have to talk to this new guy about all of this cause I think he thinks that Greg and I like each other. I have to tell the new guy that I like him, and that Greg and I are just friends. I now can see why Greg's ex-girlfriend broke up with him. Man! Well, I really have to go. Talk later. Bye!

Love,
Isabel

09/20/96

I'm just sitting here in my room. Jenny's sleeping over. We went to Nick's and watched movies. There were too many people out tonight! Holy cow! Anyway, I don't even care about who I like anymore. I'm having fun being single, so I might as well keep having fun, right? I don't know what's going on with that new guy, so if he comes around, then okay, but I'm not going to make an effort to be his girlfriend. Tomorrow is going to be so much fun. I can't fucking wait! A whole mess of people are just going to hang out and you know! Oh man. Joe and Rick are too funny. They were on the phone with us a little bit ago, laughing and totally fucked up. Dude, it was hilarious. I haven't talked to Greg. Why is it when a guy and girl are just cool being friends, one or the other ends up wanting to be more than just friends? Wow! I totally just ran out of shit to say, so I'm going to go now. See ya! Bye!

Love,

Isabel

P.S. On Wednesday, we all went back to junior high. It was a trip! I finally got to talk to Mrs. Jacobson. It was pretty cool.

10/10/96

I haven't written in here for a while. A lot of shit has happened since the last time I wrote in here. Well, I guess I should start from the beginning. Hmmm...let's see, the new guy and I are just friends. He says that he still likes me, but actions speak louder than words, right? So that explains that. Cole and I talked last night. He seems really distant. Now I know why. He somehow found out about me and this new guy. It's not like I did something wrong this time because Cole hasn't been trying too hard to ask me back out. I wish he would. But what do ya do? You can't make somebody like you. I care about him so much. I just don't know what I'm going to do. I keep getting all of these mixed-up, confusing thoughts in my mind and it's getting to the point where I can't concentrate on anything else. Oh well! Oh yeah. I'm grounded again. Me and a couple other girlfriends got caught at school for smoking a joint! Man did that suck! But 3 more days and I'm ungrounded. Funny how I got grounded when I smoke pot with my mom. Hmmmm...I went to my dad's yesterday. He doesn't know about all of this. Same old-same old.

Anyway, 1st quarter is over pretty much. I hope I got good grades. Actually, I know I did. I feel confident. Then I can show my dad and say, "see, I'm living here, smoking pot, having fun with my friends and I'm getting better grades than I did when I lived at your house. Gotta go.
Talk later.
Love,
Isabel

10/13/96
I am so excited for tomorrow to come. I'll finally be able to be ungrounded. Hopefully, I'll be able to see Cole tomorrow. Who knows with him though. I haven't the slightest idea what's been put into that boy's head, but he is acting really weird. Someone needs to drill into that head of his that I love him, and he loves me, and we belong to each other. Yesterday, I was reading letters that he has written me. One of us always end up liking one another more than the other and it always switches places. I think I need him back in my life for good. He needs me too. We'll always somehow be together. We've gone through so much together, good and bad, yet we always stay in each other's lives. I don't know. Maybe I should just let him call me and make the plans.
Well, I'm sick of writing so got to go!
Love,
Isabel

10/30/96

I just got back from driving around with Greg and Jenny. I smashed so many pumpkins. It was awesome. But anyway, we're going to go to the haunted house. Uh oh! I don't know if I can take it after Farmer Brown's Friday and Saturday! Last Sunday me and Ryan had sex again. I'm so dumb. I keep trying to tell myself that everything is going to be alright but it's not really sticking there. Oh well. We had a good time. It didn't hurt anybody, so I'll be fine. I like Cole still, but he needs to treat me better if we ever go out again. Anyway, I think I'm going to go.

Love,

Isabel

P.S. I called my dad today. Yeah, that conversation lasted 3 minutes at the most. Pretty cool, huh?

11/17/96

Cole called me yesterday, but I had to go to a wedding shower. He showed up there! But I didn't talk to him yet. I had so much fun this weekend. Friday night, Jenny, and a bunch of us went to Butterfield's. I was messed up. Then we had a sleepover. Saturday, we went shopping and then we all got messed up again. Well, I got to go. Talk later.

Love,

Isabel

11/23/96

Just sitting in this dumb ass detention for 2 fucking hours. This is all a bunch of bullshit anyway. Last night, my sister caught me smoking at Butterfield's. Now my mom is trying to ground me for it. Yeah right. I can understand why she doesn't want me to smoke. But I've smoked for at least 5 months now-maybe 1 or 2 a day and just socially...if that even. I've gone many times where I just say I don't want one. I don't see what's wrong with that. I think that's the least that I could be doing wrong. All of family practically smoked at one time in their lives and some still do. But I know that this is a phase I'm going through and no matter how much everyone is going to try to make me quit, I'm not going to stop. The only way I can quit is if I want too. If I make the choice and if I have the will power, which I know I do. So as of right now I quit smoking cigarettes forever. See I did it. It's that easy for me. No harm done and no feelings hurt. Well, I'm sick of writing so I have to go.

Love,
Isabel

11/24/96

Just sitting here in my room, sicker than a dog. Man-oh-man am I sick. Anyway, I'm pissed off at Cole because he totally ditched me. I was supposed to go over to his house one day last week, but he never called. Then he actually had the nerve to call me last night, but I just let him go right away. It was so hard to do that. I need to start standing up for myself instead of letting him walk all over me. Overall, when this shit passes over, which I know it will, I'm going to tell him I want to quit fooling around with him. I want to have a relationship with him again. I'm not going to lose hope this time. I want to be with him and only him. Every time I am with Ryan, Cole is on my mind the whole time. Afterward, I feel so guilty, like I cheated on him or something, but Cole and I aren't going out, so I'm not cheating. If we ever were together again, I would never cheat on him again. And from now on I'm going to prove to Cole that I care for him a lot. This feeling I have for him is more than I've ever felt about someone before. I think I'm falling in love with him. I'm kind of scared because I've never loved anyone before, and I know that this is real. I just hope that he's feeling the same way. I have to go now.

Love,

Isabel

12/15/96

Only 10 days until Christmas! I can't wait! It's been a while since the last time I wrote in here. Shit, I need to calm down. In the past 2 weeks, I've smoked so much weed and have been drinking so much alcohol that it's not even funny anymore. I have to go now, I think. Yeah, I do.

Talk later, bye!

Love,

Isabel

12/28/96

Just lying here in my bed, still awake, thinking about things. And you know me, I always have to write the shit down. But that's alright because I enjoy it. Anyway, my mind is mainly on Cole right now...just like always. We were together a couple nights ago. But before that we hadn't seen each other for over a month! That's a really long time for me. Almost too long. It's like I could be around him forever and still not get sick of him. I just wish he was the same way toward me. Why did I do the things I did to him? I don't think it's ever going to be the same as how it was before. I'm pretty stupid for not realizing that before. I mean when I gave him that picture of the two of us together, he just threw it in some drawer. He didn't even care to look at it. That must be telling me something, right? Plus, that board he had all those pictures of me on, he took down and now they're probably all in the garbage. He probably burnt them all. I wouldn't be surprised if he did cause he told me he was about to when we were in a fight one time. I miss him so much. I just wish I could have the guts to tell him that I love him. I'm so afraid that he's going to get scared and run away like when I said it to Ryan. At that time, Ryan was my whole world and I meant it. But what I feel for Cole is so much stronger and it feels so real and good inside. I never want this feeling to ever go away. I want him to feel the same way about me. I think maybe I should go to bed since it's 2am. I have to get

up in 7 hours, which is enough sleep for me, but I know I'm going to be up for at least another hour, thinking about Cole and about how much I love him right now. So, I guess I'll talk in here later.
Love,
Isabel
P.S. Maybe I'll dream about him because I've thought about him so much. Hmmmm....

12/29/96, 12:20am
Wow! What a night! I had so much fun. I got home a little bit ago totally tired and ready for bed but now once I lie in my bed, I start thinking again and it seems like it's harder for me to go to bed without writing something down first. Well of course, I'm thinking about Cole. I want to get together with him on New Year's Eve. I just have this feeling that we are, and it'll end up being the best time we've ever had together. I have this gut feeling that something really good is going to happen. I don't know. This is what I imagine. I'll get there and we'll set up a candlelight dinner for the two of us. We'll have an interesting conversation. Of course, I'll have a movie to watch. We'll laugh cause it'll be a good funny movie. We'll cuddle with each other on the couch. Then after the movie, we'll play cards and I'll bring over a cool boardgame that we could play. That'll take up time until midnight. We'll wait for the countdown with party hats and those noise makers. Then we'll cheer to the New Year together with a glass of Welch's grape juice. After that we'll go outside and be really loud banging pots and pans! (Just like Jenny and I did last year) Then if everything is perfect, we'll make love for the first time or we'll get really passionate in front of the fireplace, and it'll go on for a while without any interruptions. I'll tell him, I love him for the first time too. And by the time all of this ends, his parents will come home. We will both know how much we love each other and knowing we're a couple again, having no doubts and

secure thoughts of a long-lasting relationship in both our minds, while we hold hands and see the love in each other's eyes. That would be my perfect image of how that could be. I hope and I know that it'll happen. Well, I have to go to bed. Bye-bye and good night.

Love,

Isabel

P.S. I love Cole always and forever!

12/29/96

I'm just lying here listening to music and being bored. I just woke up a couple hours ago. It was nice to finally get some sleep. I don't understand me. I can't stop thinking about Cole. I don't know what's wrong with me. It hurts deep down inside to know that I've been the reason that he cried before and that he's suffered the pain of me breaking up with him and telling him about me and Ryan. I want to know what I can do to gain his trust back. I don't want him to worry anymore. I hope that when I tell him, I love him on New Year's Eve, that he'll tell me he loves me too and we'll both be happy again. Together again. Well, I suppose I should take a shower now.

Love,
Isabel

01/23/97

Wow! I've been so busy lately, I almost forgot about writing in here. Well Sub Deb is this Saturday. I can't wait. I'm so excited. I am going with a friend. But I found out that Ryan is going to Sub Deb too. I'm afraid. I don't even want to think about it. It'll be alright. Whenever I'm feeling down, I just talk to my friends, and they bring me back up again. It's pretty great. I wish life was perfect, but what are you going to do? Well, I guess I should go to bed. Goodnight. Ah ha!

Love,
Isabel

01/28/97

Oh my gosh! I couldn't believe it. My friend that I went to Sub Deb with gave me a dozen roses! It was the sweetest thing, but again I only want to be friends with a guy, and they always want something more. Anyway, I got suspended from school the rest of this week. I drank too much at Sub Deb at the dance and puked all night in the bathroom. I think I drank so much to forget that Ryan was going to be there. Talk about gossip today at school! Man-o-man. I have to go. Bye!

Love,
Isabel

Chapter Eight

11/10/96
Lying between the sheets with you
Knowing the differences that drown in our minds
Loving you without a reason
Taking me back to reality
Only to realize the loneliness
Getting over the truth
Waking up to complete silence
Separating the pieces but
Laughter turns to thunder
Running from the fear
Tearing out the insides
Melting his hunger
Desiring each other
Without a purpose
Escaping everything to
Crave the addiction
Living here beyond the limit
Trespassing the broken boundaries
Only to see the blindness
Flying away
Carrying each other to the impurity that lies ahead
Trusting that he'd care
Breaking my heart again
Changing places time after time

Dying without him on the inside
Spinning around in all different directions
Only losing control
Trying to stand in secure arms
Crying to the right one
Desperately pleading for your forgiveness
The never-ending sadness fails to leave
Screaming in the dark
Without hearing you speak
Wanting you here
Needing you near me
Sanity kicks back in
Reliving my images from the past
Time can only tell
Waiting for the happiness to come
Surviving the loudness
Suffering the beating
Loving to live in the Hell of it all

04/16/97

Well, this is it. Tonight, I'm going in front of the school board for expulsion from high school. I think I'm going to be sick. What if I do? My life will be shattered into so many pieces. It's a major turning point, that's for sure. Exactly one hour until the hearing now. I don't think I've ever felt so many things all at once. Wow! I never really worried about it until now. How did I ever get to where I'm at in the first place? I could've totally avoided the two incidences. But they've already happened, and I can't go back and change anything now, so what's the use in feeling sorry for myself, right? We'll see how things go. I'm not touching a drip of alcohol or a shred of weed for a very long time. Everyone I've talked too seems to be on my side and wants to help me and defend me in any way they can. I also have God on my side, and I thank Him for this. Wondering what I did? Well, first I got caught smoking pot nearby school. Then, I got caught being drunk at Sub Deb. Dumb, dumb, dumb. I'm going to go for now.

Love,

Isabel

04/28/97

"Memories of You"

I remember your bright smile when you'd look at me
I remember your soft touch and the way it felt
I remember your put-together appearance
I remember your sweet words that poured into my heart
I remember how you'd do anything for me
I remember your ways and your philosophies
I remember the long hours we'd spend just holding each other
I remember when you'd gently brush my cheek as we'd kiss
I remember the butterflies I'd get every time you whispered "I love you"
And how I knew you meant it
I remember the way you'd look at me when you thought I was sleeping
I remember the red roses you gave me
And how sweet they smelled
I remember looking at them and thinking of you
I remember your certain smell that would linger in my nose after we'd
touch
I remember how happy we were just being together
I remember that sparkle in your eyes
I remember you

May 1997
"Three Free Wings in Yellow"
Take away my soul
To face the rage
Fearing the light
Unlock the cage
Underneath my shadows
Empty the jar of hearts
Free me from the burn
Before the fire starts
Take the stars
Balancing on my fingertips
Peel my skin and leave the ash
See my red eyes
Existing beneath the crash
Off the boundaries and into my world
Tip toeing your way closer to my pulse
Just to realize your intention is false
Look at the blue vein
Twirl it in an oval
Run from the insane
Hide your face in the darkness
Again, I awake
Seeing three free wings in yellow
Fly high away with me
I dance to his melody
His embrace upon me
Burn the crackle
Blow out the flame
Hardly different from the same
Flying lower
Sunken beneath the strife

Munch the marrow
Breathe the life
Stitch my dress
Color my picture
Blush my cheek
Undo my zipper
Pull over my sheet
Kiss my neck
Sing my lullaby
Look into my eyes
Sleep in my arms all night
Want me
And hold me real tight
In the morning we'll both see
The beautiful butterflies flying free

05/02/97

Hey! Just sitting on my bed, lying down. Felt like writing. Well, a lot of stuff has happened since the last time I wrote in here. First of all, I'm still in high school. I got expelled, but I'm going through the Bridges program, which isn't bad at all. It's actually helping me out. I still get to go to most of my classes so it's still pretty much back to normal. God helped me through everything and I'm so thankful for that. I've been attending a youth group at a local church on Wednesdays. I love it there. It helps me out a lot. I've also met a lot of new people! I haven't touched weed or alcohol since last Wednesday. I know I'll be keeping that up. God will help me. And I thank Him every day for that. My grades are getting higher, and everything is going great in my life right now. Even me and dad's relationship is going great. I told him everything and he acted the exact opposite I thought he was going too. Well, I'm going to bed now.
Love,
Isabel

06/30/97

It seems to be a little more different every time I want to write in here because there is no time. I had so much to say but once I open the pages.... I don't know. Anyway, I just got a job about a month ago. Saving up for a car. Going to driver's ed. I've been having the best summer so far! I'm going to Summerfest this Thursday and Friday. I guess that's all I had to say. Talk later.

Love,
Isabel

07/08/97

Sometimes I really don't understand guys. I talked to Cole last night down by the lake and he seemed like he wanted to get back with me. I'm not calling him. If he wants me that bad, he can call me! I don't think we are going to get back together though. He has no time for me. Well maybe I'm going to start not having any time for him either. Well, I have to go.

Love,
Isabel

07/17/97

Wow! I can't believe it! Cole and I might be getting back together again. We both have good intentions. I'm not going to keep my hopes up. But I think he's finally, after a year, learned to regain my trust again. I'm so happy. I just know a lot is going to happen to us in the future. I need someone in my life that will keep me stable. He's the one! He has been. I just hope the time comes soon. Anyway, I'm really anxious for this weekend to end. I'm grounded cause I didn't call and check in when I was supposed to. Well, I have to go.

Love,

Isabel

07/27/97

Just sitting here being really bored. Reading through all of these entries. It's all so crazy. It's like I remember having those feelings and being in those situations but it's non-existent now. I really am sick of writing in here. My hands are starting to cramp up and so is my back. So goodbye!
Love,
Isabel

Chapter Nine

Spirit

08/14/97

Take me to that place you carried me before

Take me to the place where my wings can soar

Creeping through the blackness

Jumping over the walls

Lift my inner soul that glows in front of you

To see the rainbow in the waterfalls

The snow-white unicorns grazing in the shadows

Whisper the scent to fill the hollowed inside

Fill it with grape, sparkled bubbles

Shine your sunlight against my soft skin

With my silver-tipped eyelashes

Look at the glow and wander into the night

Spin the world and let the universe go round

But just for today do me a favor

And spit on my face

08/13/97
I hope to love you
When you love me
To love only you
Your touch, your kiss
Again, and again
The others break my heart
But you've always been there
Unnoticed
How can I treat you the way they treat me?
Knowing how it feels
Yearning for a simple treasure called love
Just like you

08/13/97

I'm a simple girl

Not much for someone to make me happy

I'm a girl with wings

Wanting to soar high

Only to see

To touch

Another butterfly

08/15/97
When you see all the hate and sorrow
In this world
Wishing for a brighter tomorrow
The faith in Him
Slowly decreases
When you see all the miracles and happiness
In this world
Don't ask any more questions
Have faith

08/15/97
The potion for love is
Within yourself
To believe and trust in your own
Independence
And when a smile turns
Into laughter
The meaning stands
Right in front of you

08/15/97

"Aspiration"

To others it hurts
But for some the pain surrenders
No one is invisible
Disappearing from the tank
That empties out the waste
Surrounding us with lace
The ray shines in black eyes
Blinding them
Here it opens the rose petal
Blooming by itself
Each thorn pricks the wound
The petals fall
The vines wrap around our ankles
Grabbing our souls
To the pit of our hearts
Where does this cupid bury itself?
The wind blows away the dust
Carrying us away together
The clouds fill our breath
As we exhale the thunderstorms
It locks in the brokenness
So, we can become one
To others it hurts
But for some the pain surrenders

"Untitled"
And the way he makes me feel
As you stare into my crying eyes
I don't speak a word
Holding the sadness inside
How will I know if you love me?
Will you ever love me?
The touch of my pulse
Creating no beat
Just the tears empty out
Sinking below...
And the way he makes me feel...

09/29/97
"The Stranger"
Outside the windowpane
A man sits on the curb
A brief thought of her arises in his mind
He awaits the presence of a being
The dark surrounds him
Only the light of the man on the moon
Silence creates a repetitious melody of yesterday
Slowly, his lips inhale the drug
As his soul departs from his body
Flashing lights appear in the distance
For a brief moment
He lifts his head up to the endless stars
A napkin and ink float in his hand
The man writes down
"happiness"
A crooked smile stretches across his face
Her beauty sparkles before him
Beneath his eyes
Realizing no need at all
Having everything in the palm of his hand
Outside the windowpane
A man stands at dawn
He steps in another direction
Searching for the beginning
He hums a soft melody of long ago
With grace
Looking up with dignity
The man disappears forever
With only happiness in his palm.

Chapter Ten

Tyler
10/16/97

It seems it has been a while since I've written an actual entry, so I thought I 'd write in my spare hours. I'm so content, it seems, with my life. I got a job, keeping up with school and have met the sweetest guy in my heart. Tyler is the best thing that's ever happened to me. I deserve it too, with all the bullshit I dealt with in the past. Every time I see him an instant smile arises on my face. I'm so happy. I'm not going to ruin this. Maybe this is the one. I'm not sure. I know I care for him more than anyone. I know he cares for me too. We're both scared that something might happen to our relationship, like others in our past. I hope that despite anything that would happen, we have lots of fun together and be happy. That's all I really want. But in that case, doesn't everyone? I'm so lucky to have found him. We miss each other even though we've been apart for only a couple of days. Right there is a good example of a good quality in a relationship. Not everyone feels that way. I'm never taking this for granted. Hopefully that will keep us together for a long time.
Well, I guess I had better get to bed.
Love,
Isabel

11/11/97

I talked to Cole tonight on the phone. We had a real interesting conversation. I really wish he isn't the way he is. I don't know. But he asked me how Tyler and I are doing? I was very surprised he asked me that! So, I told him the truth. I told him that our relationship couldn't be better, and I couldn't be any happier. It seemed like he had so much more to tell me, then he actually did, but you know how that goes. Well Tyler decided to get a job with his ex-girlfriend, which I wasn't too thrilled about. And he knows it. I know I'm not overreacting about this, but isn't it a little awkward? He wouldn't like it if I would've accepted that job with Cole, now, would he? Doubtful. This has nothing to do with jealously or trust. It has to do with plain, old-fashioned respect. Well, I have to go have a smoke, so I'll write in here later.

Love,
Isabel

12/29/97

I am so happy. Nobody could be happier than me right now. I'm so much in love with Tyler. He's my everything, my world. We have such a good time together. I know he's my soulmate. We'll last forever. And we're the only ones that truly believe this. We're the only ones that know the truth and our fate. Every time I see him smile or hear him laugh, my heart beats so fast. I love him so much. This relationship is so real compared to any previous ones. This is definitely true love. I finally understand what it's like to have a long, happy, strong, and loving relationship with someone. Now that I do, it's like no one could ever possibly take that away from me. I never want to let this go. It will never end. I've never felt like this right now. Just lying here in my bed, I feel as if I'm missing something. In my mind, I know it's him holding me all through the night forever. I'm so sure of this. (588-968)

Love,

Isabel

01/13/98

Tyler and I had a real good quality talk tonight. He makes me so happy.
I wonder if we'll last forever? It's only been 4 months, but I have this
strong feeling about our love that grows inside of my soul. Cole called
me again on my answering machine. I'm ready to just call him and tell
him to get over it already. Obviously, it was easy for him in July, so why
isn't it now? I want to tell Tyler that he called again but I'm afraid that
he'll want to start some shit with him and get in trouble with his PO.
There's no way I'll ever risk him going to jail for anyone. If he ever had
to go to jail, I don't know what I'd do. I'm so sick of all the shit his damn
family put him through. I wish he'd just get an apartment so we
wouldn't have to worry about anything. I love him so much. He's my
world and probably always will be. I'm so excited for Sub Deb! It's going
to be too much fun. Last Sub Deb sucked. Probably cause of who I went
with. I don't know. Well, I'm going to go to sleep so I can wake up and
go to another boring ass day of school! Yeah! Well at least I don't have
to work!
Love,
Isabel
P.S. Tyler + Isabel Forever!

02/13/98

Tonight, I have the strangest feeling. It's as if I see my whole future waiting in front of me. But yet it's so hard to grasp it. I've been writing in the journal for 2 years now and so much has changed me, inside and out. There are still so many blank sheets to write on but yet they aren't filled. I have so many thoughts yet to be written, but I can't seem to find myself. Two years ago, I thought I was going to be dead. Two years ago, I thought I had everything all figured out, but I only have a tiny piece of everything. I'm only 16, but life has gone by so fast already. Two years ago, I would've never even begun to imagine that I'd be where I am now. I would've never thought that I'd find the sweetest guy in the whole world. I've finally found happiness in someone that has found happiness in me. It's all a dream. I pinch myself. I wake up to reality. My thoughts are scattered, maybe not meaning anything, but they mean something to me now. They always will. There's a reason for everything. There's a reason for this moment right now. Maybe I'll never find out what it is. It all seems like it's moving too fast. Life shouldn't go by so quickly. We should have longer hours and days. Then time would move slower. Or maybe it's all a figment of my imagination. But if life slowed down, there might be too much time for us to spare. If God didn't have so many decisions for us to make and so many roads to choose from, we'd all lose this game. That is all we play. We're sometimes playing defense and sometimes offense. Sometimes we're the victims of an irrational society where everyone spits on respect. In a world I'm growing up in, times get harder and harder. The more you try to stay out of trouble, the more pressure creeps up into your nightmares. Dreams are intense. And when you're in your deepest sleep, is when you realize there is no place I'd rather be. The grass is green, the sky is blue, and the clouds are black sometimes. Two years from now, I wonder where I'll be? I know I won't be at Harvard, studying my ass off, to be some kind of prosecutor that everyone would hate. Only to get stuck with an OJ case and going to my mansion, sitting at the end of a 30-foot-long dinner table, reading a newspaper, and occasionally asking my husband at the other end to pass the salt. No! This is not going to happen. I think I'm burned out with thoughts, so I'll write in here some other time.

Love,
Isabel

02/18/98

Everything is really going great in my life right now. Tyler and I just got a job together. I hope I like it there. I get paid to start at $5.50/hour plus 10% commission. So anyway, I've been feeling like everything is fitting right into place in my life right now. I finally found happiness! It's all moving so fast though. I'm growing up so fast and I'm only 16. I kept trying to tell myself that, but I've gone through so much already. It's kind of scary to see what else I must face in the future. What mistakes will I make? What will I be doing? Who will I be with? What kind of happiness will find me? I guess I'll have to wait for that time to come. Until then, I hope I can please everyone around me and only wish for the best for myself. I've already gone through a lot. I've seen so much. Well time to go to bed.

Love,
Isabel

Chapter Eleven

Letters from Tyler

Isabel,

Hey babe! I hope you are thinking about me right now. I thought I'd write and tell you how much, how I very much care about you. I was really upset and hurt by what you said to me tonight. I can't believe that you feel that way. If that is what you think than you are totally wrong. I will have to prove it to you then. It's too bad that I have to prove myself to you. I stopped all that stuff, so I wouldn't hurt special people like you. You are way too special to me. I wouldn't do anything to hurt you. You mean way too much to me. I'm more scared than you are. Yes, I am, so don't argue. I have very strong feelings for you. I'm crazy about you Isabel. You make me so happy. Every time I look at you or are around you, I feel more content and more comfortable than I've ever felt. There is just something about you that makes everyone so bright and cheerful. You are a beautiful person on the outside, but you are the most beautiful person on the inside. You are everything that I have been looking for. Someone to share my stories and my problems. Someone I can trust and who cares. Someone I can always hangout with and have fun. I wouldn't want anything to come between us. I like to be able to share anything with you. When I look into your captivating eyes, I see a world of excitement that I can't wait to explore and learn from. I can't think of anyone I would rather share my life with. Don't compare me to anyone or anything you've heard. Everyone deserves a fair chance. That is all I ask. I accept you for who and what you are. Please do the same for me. Judge me by what I do and how I am now. Forget the past, I'm trying too. I want to be able to give you anything you want or need. You deserve it more than anyone. You are the sweetest, most sincere person I know. You have so many wonderful qualities that make you so special. Any guy would be lucky to have you. I'm just glad that I was the lucky one. You won't ever have anything to worry or be scared about. I promise. I don't ever break my promises either. I am just scared that I will lose you and I just got you. I care about you very deeply. Don't ever forget that. Think of me always. Love,

Tyler

Isabel,

How are you sweetheart? I thought I would write since I haven't written in a long time. Besides, I can't talk to you or see you right now and I can't get you out of my mind. So, I thought I'd tell you how much I missed you. This was such a long weekend. I just wanted to hear your beautiful voice. I can't wait to look into those hypnotizing eyes that make me melt and my heart tingle. You are so amazing that I can't stand being apart from you. Everything about you makes me feel like the luckiest guy in the whole world. I didn't get any sleep this whole weekend. Well, hmm, I stopped writing for a while to try to get you off my mind to focus on other things, but that didn't work. So, I started writing again. Not being able to get you off my mind made me realize something. It made me realize just how strong my love for you is and what a big part of my life you are. It also made me realize that words alone can't express how much I love you and care for you. I had this weird feeling since Friday, I think it's because I can't be with you this weekend. If I get this feeling about not seeing you for 3 days, then what would I do if I couldn't be with you at all. So, I figure we are going to have to be together forever.

Love always,

Tyler

Chapter Twelve

Lust

"My Promise"
Forever my heart will beat for you
No one will ever tear this love
Our fate will hold us together
I promise....
Knowing our souls are together as one
My love grows stronger every day
Like a sunlit horizon, your smile brightens up my world
I promise....
You are my first love
My true love
My greatest strength for always
I promise....
In your arms
I'm safe and secure
I'll never slip away
I promise....
Hearing your heart beat next to mine
I'd give my all just to be with you
To hold you all night long
I promise....
No matter what it takes

I'd risk my everything just for you
I'll stand by your side till time stands still
I promise....
My future is with you
Our lives we can share together
And I promise you
That will last a lifetime.
When you're feeling alone
I will always appear
Take my hand and never fear
With minds alike
Together we think
As you stare in my eyes
Without a blink
Take me to our place
You carried me before
Take me to our place
Where my wings can soar
Taste my sugared lips
Hug your face into my hips
Shine your sunlight
Against my soft skin
Bury yourself deep within
Breathe in my lovely scent
As you become more and more content
Look into my blinding eyes
Whispering, to me, my lullabies
With my silver-tipped eyelashes
Brushing the dust out
Tears vanish forever without a doubt
Press upon my breasts
Up against the picture

Blush my cheek
Undo my zipper
As we fly free
Your embrace is upon me
Take me as I am
Trust the words of my heart
And together we belong
Never apart

You've made these days so special to me. Never do I want this feeling to leave. Just sitting here, thinking about you, makes me realize how much love I hold inside. Every time I give myself to you, I know that I'm fortunate
Fortunate to have your arms wrapped around my body
And I give you my all....

As I share with you my thoughts
As I become closer to your soul
With my eyes
Your smile, I'll always see
Feeling your embrace
Touching you against my face
Looking into your eyes
Revealing myself from a disguise
Kissing my lips
Burying your face in between my hips
Holding your hand
Knowing where we stand
Giving you my all
Preventing ourselves from the fall
Loving your ways
Remembering these days
Smiling when we stare
Realizing you'll always be there
Seeing we're meant for each other
Knowing you're my best friend and lover
Timing the days together
Capturing our future fate forever
Wanting our love to stay strong
Having to stand where I belong
Lift me up
Carry me high
And together we'll last until existence disappears
Until our separate rivers dry out

01/11/98
"You're the One"
You're the one who showed me love
Lying on a pillow of bliss
Embracing each other
Thinking to myself
"You're too good to be true. Someone loves me in return?"
My dreams came true
The wish we both wish together
Stays strong
As long as my heart beats, it beats for you
You're the one for me
Always
I see the reflection of our future
In your eyes
We'll exist together in happiness
Your smile keeps my days bright
Your strong hands hold our fate
The candle will burn forever
Our rivers will flow as one
My soul holds yours
You're the one that I'll love
Always
Belonging with you
As you carry me higher
When life brings me lower
Kiss my eternal soul
And we'll both float through the clouds
You're the one that I'll be with forever
I love you.

02/09/98
"In a Heartbeat"
In a heartbeat
My empty hands would give you everything
My lips would give you all the advice you need
I'd fill my head with your words
And believe in them
I'll believe in you
My heavy shoes
Would run anywhere for you
My blind eyes
Would search the world for you
My shoulder will be there
For you to lean on
My ears will listen to you
Whenever you're in need
My heart and soul
Will always be present
Even when my body isn't
I'll stand by you forever
Because I'm so proud to say that I'm yours.

Toss the tears that
Trickle till twilight
Taste the tempting tongue
That teases their thrill
Tonight, together in a trance
Till the termination of time.

03/07/98
"The Horizon"
To tempt the desire
Bare flesh appears
Empty hearts fill
Nights are clear
Whirl wind blows upon us
To the depths of our minds
Together we endure
Untouchable times now felt
Existence faces our future
Souls collapse into warm hands
The smile sees light
Shadows fade
Hips touch as the sunrise appears beyond the horizon.

03/15/98
"My Angel"
When you flew down
I fell on my knees
Your soul sank into my heart
You're my love...
You're my angel...

03/16/98

"I Am"

I have long brown hair
Bright blue eyes
My skin is soft
My smile is warm
I have a widow's peak
I have a birth mark on my thigh
I bite my nails
I crack my knuckles
I make mistakes
I am honest
I am selfish
I have an answer for everything
I am happy
I cry sometimes
I give good advice
I talk too much
I am strong-willed
I fear the dark
I fear to be alone
I love butterflies
I love green
I am sensitive
I am grateful
I am me
And he loves me for that.

As I lay here, just another night, I keep thinking about you so much. It's as though I'm a different person. I've changed to the point when I confuse myself sometimes. I don't know where I'm headed, and I don't care right now. I just want to hold on to these memories in my life right now. I've gone through so much and I'm so excited to see what will be waiting for me in 10 years. What will I have accomplished? But I'm here now and that's all that matters to me. Nothing in this world can change that right now. I fell in love 10 months ago with a guy I thought was "the one for me." Today I broke up with him, not caring or regretting it, not scared that I made a huge mistake. I thought I needed to make a change right now and that's exactly what I did. Now we'll see what happens now that I've let go of a very big part of my life, a big part of my heart and soul. I wish I could hold onto the first days we shared forever. There's not a day that I regret spending my time with him. But now I'm going to choose the right paths. Life will take me anywhere I let it. Anything can get worse if I let it. I've chosen to ride the rollercoaster. Live life to its fullest. Learn from the mistakes. Tomorrow can always be a better day if I allow it to be. It's all in my mind. I can take control of it. I can make my life do whatever I want it to do. I'm not afraid, I have no fears.

05/06/98

This will be my last entry. I feel as if I'm finishing a chapter of my life. It's a small chapter that has let me learn from some of the mistakes I've made and understand the decisions that should've been made. I wish to start out my next journal with a new perspective on life. Reading back on this will give me a remembrance of good and bad memories. I have gone through a lot and have and still am teaching myself how to deal with the realities of life. I will choose the right paths and learn so much more about what life is all about. I'm so glad that I went through and experienced all of the things I did. It made me a stronger person. I know I'm not the only one. I'm not alone in this world. I will create my own happiness and I'm grateful for God's presence.

Love,

Isabel

Chapter Thirteen

Live

12/05/98

The fingers grab me

Holding me back

Suffocating my indulgence

Take my soul

Life won't challenge me

We all see the eyes

Staring at my sweets

Falling farther into clumsy arms

Break my fall

Catch my breath

Please! Avoiding absence

Gaining strength

Prick your wound

Death approaches you

I am immortal

Hold my hand

Fly with me

No more pain

Float on the wings

Free at last

1999

"The Addiction"

To help the confusion
My mind creates the illusion
Never again will it settle
Finally, I creep inside
So that I can crawl and hide
Into the massive shadows
The skin, so sweet
As our bodies meet
Underlying the world beneath
Cradle the stars into our palms
Staring at it calmly
To disappoint our minds
Desperation embeds us
Our souls tangle in lust
Satisfying the hunger
Madness slips through your head
Only melting instead of letting it escape
Feel the pressure
Find the buried treasure
Come find the jewel
Fly away near no one
Feel my tongue
Hurt me, but never suffer
As we hear the thunder
Let the rain drown us
Deep into the core
I will need more
Of the crave
The addiction

"Untitled"
I feel your presence
I hear your voice
My soul shakes
As my heart beats
I see your silhouette
You exist, but not here
I taste your lips
I breathe your breath
I smell your scent
The need is what I fear
I can't hold you
I can't touch you
Do you still exist?
Think of me
Infinite days
I will kneel
Kissing the skin
Take me
Carry me away
Fly with me
The shadows will keep us real
My throat won't fill with pain
My eyes won't burn with rain
My mind won't go insane
Only if I hear your name
Only if I fly with you
You are my angel

01/11/2000

"My Angel"

Vicious mentality creeps in

The white doves sleep

The black crows awaken

Curly vines wrap around my veins

The being appears

Screaming voices in the distance

No one hears

The smoke erases my memory

Still, a thought arises

It's him, again

Breaking past the wall

Escaping the fear of the fall

There's no end

The beginning lingers

Conquer the bitter

Sweet is only left

Then he disappears again

Meaningless destruction

Overpower him

Overcome the ache

Touch me

Feel me, again

Even if it hurts

Love won't eat it

Love swallows' dignity

Corrupt minds swirl

Forgetting the rest of the world

Focus on my body

Focus on me

Soul's touch

Ponder my last thought
It's him, again
Time doesn't exist
No one does
He erased my soul
He erased my mind
He erased the sweet
He erased me
And then he held my hand
Touched his soft lips against mine
And disappeared into the sunshine
Time is endless
My angel that once breathed
Flies invincible

01/25/2000

"Reflection"

Time heals wounds
Wounds stain life
Life swallows' minds
Minds trap souls
Souls light fire
Fire burns pity
Pity lies alone
Alone fears truth
Truth swirls lies
Lies keep secrets
Secrets melt smiles
Frowns wrinkle skin
Skin hides hearts
Hearts beat music
Music needs rhythm
Rhythm demands dance
Dance frees spirits
Spirits grasp angels
Angels fly immortal
Immortality desires existence
Existence sharpens reality
Reality reflects dreams
Dreams fade reality
Reality reflects dreams
Dreams fade reality...

"Only I"
As I glance at this woman
As beautiful as a butterfly
The impurities surface
Distinctive flaws magnify
The eyes such a sky blue
The smile as bright as the stars
Yet the hands so fragile
As they quiver, while feeling the scars
And on the inside the gratefulness appears
The spirit enlightens the heart
Thankful God created an amazing piece of art
The intensity grows slowly
As I come to realize
The endless amounts of selfishness and sin
That remain in my eyes
Yet the honesty runs through the vein
The heart so pure
While the mind slowly goes insane
A touch of reality
A taste of bittersweet
The friends of loyalty
The enemies of deceit
The puzzle of life remains
As I look up toward the sky
Only one woman
Only one mind to nourish
Only I

"Looking Into the Eyes of a Stranger"
When the night is black
She sees clearer
As the raindrops fall
She is happier
As the sun rises in the far distance
A smile appears on His face
His eyelashes touch its' rays
A rainbow appears
And He finds the end of it
She enjoys dancing with shadows
He climbs and struggles
But reaches the highest mountain top
She crawls slowly as a caterpillar would
He turns into a butterfly
And has strong yellow wings
Then suddenly a star drops from the sky
And touches both of them
He kisses her softly
The softer He kisses her
The more afraid she is that He'll break her
With His wings
He holds her hand
Lifts her up
And carries her away
Into the sky on a rose petal
As His lips touch the sky
He appears to kiss the red-hot sun
The sky becomes a pinkish blue
Then a purplish blue
As the night becomes darker
The sparks fly throughout the sky

To create all the tiny stars, we see at midnight
My heart shatters
My soul weakens as the sun sets
He leaves the moon behind
I feel the shadows
Pressing against my chest
Then my eyes gleam with the moonlight
And I'm happy again
I slowly daze into the clouds
And see Him once more
He kisses the sky to create more stars
Sand blows into a sea of floating starfish
They dance about onto the shore
My fingernails get dirty, and my body feels heavy
My thought becomes too weak to speak
I kiss Him
We float once again
Along with the tide
He kisses the sky to hide the stars
The seagulls come out to kiss the sun
Peace twirls in the salty air
The sky turns orange and pink
Diamonds reflect
On a glimmering ocean at dawn
And I am complete

Chapter Fourteen

Faith

The above journal entries and poems that I wrote are from the years 1997-2000...when I was age 15 to 19. I am 42 now. Prior to these entries, I had already been molested at age 10 and again at age 13 by a family member. Also, a lot of bullying from other kids occurred on and off throughout school in many different ways. Fights in school. Expulsion from school for drugs and alcohol. I took a half bottle of aspirin at age 14 in a suicide attempt, which just got me really sick, and no one ever found out about it. I had a full suicide plan at the age of 15, which was going to occur with a gun and on the nearby railroad tracks. God was present in my life and the next morning when I woke up, I knew that and never had another suicide attempt again. I was date raped at the age of 16, while I was high and drunk. I kept saying "no" the whole time and he wouldn't stop. I was completely helpless. That event may be part of the reason why I always needed to be in control of everything from that point on. I was involved in a bad car accident involving drugs and alcohol at age 16, when I went through the windshield. I struggled as a young adult with many different drugs and alcohol. This was a result from growing up in a household with alcoholics and drug addicts.

I was homeless at age 18 when I moved out of state with that guy, Tyler, that I couldn't live without at the end of my journal entries. Turns out he was full of rage because of his own family problems and took it out on me. I was the victim of mental abuse that if I didn't get out of that situation, it would've easily turned into physical abuse. He started to throw things at me and destroy things in our apartment before we were evicted. I understand the circle of violence, fighting and then making up and making excuses for him, thinking it was mostly my fault, then repeat. Or thinking the good outweighs the bad, especially when he was so sweet to me the next day. Or not leaving because of being afraid to be alone.

I remember when I finally moved back home and chose to get out of that situation, he stalked me at my work, just showed up there one day, when I thought he was still out of state. I took him out to the parking lot to talk with him. He told me he can't live without me and was going to kill himself if I didn't go back to him. I told him it was over, and he needed to get help. We went back and forth for a while after that day, but eventually the relationship dissolved, and it was not easy to break away from him. If you are in this situation, go talk to a professional, sometimes you need some help from others and that's ok. If you have children with him, don't stay because of them...LEAVE because of them. They deserve to grow up in a stable home. Otherwise, they may repeat the same pattern in their own lives. **BREAK THE CYCLE. YOU CAN DO IT!!!**

After I moved back home, I decided to go to college. I had my first beautiful baby boy. Heartaches on and off with 2 miscarriages and a divorce. I went through a divorce and was a single parent and still managed to accomplish graduating college summa cum laude (highest honor)! I took out loans and paid for school all on my own! While working full time, I would study after my son went to bed every night and on the weekends. It took time but it can be done, no excuses, just sacrifice and perseverance. Then I met my true love and soulmate and had a beautiful baby girl. Still dealing with life's struggles, our baby girl had to have 2 brain surgeries due to epilepsy when she was only a 1 ½ years old. She has special needs, feeding tube, therapies and learning to talk. With lots of prayers and support, she is doing great now, seizure free.

I have dealt with my own battle of depression and anxiety, which is a continual journey through life. But that is life. Learning from mistakes. Building true relationships with those around you that nurture your soul. Learning coping skills for the hard times. And building a foundation of love, trust, respect, and compromise with others. The choice to live can sometimes be the toughest decision during the hard times. But seeking help is the first step. I started going to counseling in junior high school and continued with it throughout my life. Talking about your problems with a professional is not a taboo. It's ok. We all have problems and need some extra help sometimes. Some of us still use alcohol and drugs to mask the problems, forget about them for a while. But that is not a healthy coping skill. Those behaviors will filter over to your own children and starts a learned cycle that continues on into their lives.

There are infinite resources online that can help you get through problems you may be having. **Don't give up. You are not alone**. There are many people that are having the same struggles right now. The hard times in life help you gain more strength in life. You get stronger the more you fight. God and prayer always guided me through life, you will never be alone. It's easier to dwell on the negative things in life. Write down all the positive things in your life and look at it every time you think a negative thought throughout the day. Encourage yourself to think positive thoughts and be grateful that we have another day to live. We all have at least one sense to enjoy, our sight, our smell, our touch, our hearing, our taste. If you can't see the sun, feel it on your skin. If you can't hear the music, dance to your own beats. If you can't smell the flowers, pick them for someone else to enjoy. If you can't taste, see the sun, feel the touch of someone's hug and dance to the music. Squeeze the good out of your life <u>every single day</u>. It's there, **you just have to find it**. It's waiting for you; **you just have to seek it.** Always give more than you receive. **The past already happened. The future doesn't exist yet. So, focus on the present...today...right now...**close your eyes...take a deep breath through your nose real slow, then blow out your breath through your mouth real slow and repeat multiple times daily, especially on a bad day. Meditation and yoga can help you to focus on the present. For example, when you eat a hamburger, smell it, hold it, take a small bite, taste the bite, eat slowly...this is really hard to do when you are hungry, but it is an example of how you can practice living in the present moment verses the alternative of eating it quickly while watching tv. Another example is when you are having a conversation with someone else, practice to make eye contact, really listen to what they are saying, think about your answer, then determine if you need to respond or not.

Thinking about life in a positive light will change your life:

There is always a positive out of a negative.

You can turn anxiety into faith.

You can turn depression into hope.

You can turn fear into bravery.

You can turn fear of death into value of life.

You can turn rage into peace and forgiveness.

You can turn weakness into strength.

You can turn a mistake into knowledge.

God will be your voice, as you may not know you have one yet.

God only exists in the present.

No matter what you have been though or going through, family molestation, date rape, mental or physical abuse, abandonment, miscarriage, death of loved one, homelessness, addiction to drugs or alcohol, mental illness or even heartbroken from a breakup/divorce...**YOU ARE NOT ALONE.** Reach out to a friend, neighbor, a local church, a shelter and give your fears to God. He will carry you out of the struggles but not before you learn something from it. You may not know it at the time or ever, but usually when you look back, if you've been able to recover from one of your struggles, realize that the struggles can make you stronger and helps you to continue to survive.

I AM GRATEFUL, I AM COURAGEOUS, I AM STRONG, I AM WORTHY. (Repeat this to yourself throughout the day or create your own phrase) When you think positively, it draws in positivity. If you or a loved one are struggling with life, please get help today. Suicide and Crisis Lifeline (free, confidential, 24/7), go to 988lifeline.org or call/text 988

www.activeminds.org[1], text BRAVE to 741-741

National Domestic Violence Hotline (free, confidential, 24/7), go to thehotline.org or call 1-800-799-SAFE or text START to 88788

Loveisrespect.org or call 1-800-331-9474 or text LOVEIS to 22522

If you are a teenager, go to teenline.org or call 1-800-852-8336 or text TEEN to 839863

SAMHSA's (substance abuse and mental health services) National Helpline, go to samhsa.gov or call 1-800-662-HELP (4357)

---

1. http://www.activeminds.org